Amberdale

and the Railway Which Runs Through It

PHILIP HARVEY

FONTHILL

This book is dedicated to Caroline, whose encouragement has never wavered, and without whose support Amberdale would never have been built.

www.fonthillmedia.com
office@fonthillmedia.com

First published in the United Kingdom
and the United States of America 2021

British Library Cataloguing in Publication Data:
A catalogue record for this book is available from the British Library

ISBN 978-1-78155-849-2

Typeset in Minion Pro
Printed and bound in England

Contents

Introduction

This is not a book about model railways, nor is it a book showing how to build them. It is simply a collection of photographs of one particular and very personal model that will, I hope, be of interest to railway modellers generally and to others who are not familiar with the hobby.

Model railways come in all sorts of shapes and sizes, from some that fit on coffee tables to those filling large halls, from precise masterpieces reproducing every detail of real locations to those set out (until bedtime) on the carpet. The scope of the hobby is so wide that it is, perhaps, worth defining just what we mean by a model railway, before going on to explain what sort of model railway this book is about. What links the meticulous accuracy of the models in, say, the Pendon Museum to a toy train set and to the great variety of models in between, and where does the one illustrated in this book fit in? Does a 'model railway' have to include a railway at all, and is any model that does a 'model railway'? Pendon is a good example of this ambiguity. Should the vale scene be described as a model railway—the railway is a minor element in the overall landscape—and might it not be so described even if it had no railway at all? After all, it is built to a popular railway modelling scale and includes features common to most model railways.

A model railway must certainly include a railway of some sort, but again, the term is ambiguous. Trams run on a railway, but a model tramway is not a model railway. A model railway must surely feature railway trains, as that term is generally understood, and crucially, the trains must be capable of being worked and of being able to move along the tracks. The train set laid out on the carpet, running round in circles, is undoubtedly a model railway; a static display in a museum, however extensive and detailed, is not.

However a model railway might be defined, and however wide the scope of that description, 'a model of a railway' is something rather more particular. Such a model reflects that a railway runs from one place to another and provides for the interchange of traffic between them. A model of a single station is not, in this context, a model of a railway, though I concede that it might be described as a model railway. The model described in this book is of a railway, one which runs from one end to the other, calling at various places in between.

Prior to the current popularity of single-station layouts, which really stems back to the 1950s, the traditional model railway often comprised a convoluted network of tracks linking as many stations as could be fitted into the available space. Edward Beal's West Midland was a classic example, but despite its fictional history and its extended route mileage, it was not, in my view, a model of a railway. Railways do not follow complex, devious, and repetitive paths between places immediately adjacent to each other, as the West Midland did; they follow the most practical direct route between places some distance apart. Neither do they run round in circles, nor run alongside numerous parallel routes leading to separate destinations.

A variation on this theme might be illustrated by Peter Denny's Buckingham line. While this impressive model also linked a number of places together by a direct line of railway, there was no separation between them other than by an abrupt scenic break. Buckingham had several stations but no railway. A model of a railway, as I am defining it, has always been something of a rarity. The best-known example must surely be the Madder Valley, built by the late John Ahern.

While my interest in model railways was kindled by Edward Beal, and in particular by his book *Railway Modelling in Miniature* given to me by my father in 1947, it was discovering the Madder Valley a few years later that really inspired me and continues to do so. Photographs of the West Midland were impressive, but they were pictures of what was clearly just an extensive model railway. While I enthused over them, I think I unconsciously accepted that they bore little resemblance to the real world. A model railway, indeed any model, is surely intended to represent or at least reflect the full-size reality, but in Beal's pictures, there was no attempt to conjure up any such impression, either in the models themselves or in the pictures, and they were lacking on that score.

But Ahern's photos were a revelation. Here were models of a recognisable world that looked real, which really did reflect reality. Here was a model of a railway that ran through a credible landscape connecting separate communities together. He showed how such models could be built from everyday materials without exceptional expertise, their scope limited only by the imagination, not the depth of one's pocket.

This was the sort of railway that appealed, and something that it might be possible to emulate one day. The seeds of Amberdale were sown. After extensive trial and error as a teenager (Railway of the Month, *Railway Modeller*, December 1957), the first Amberdale models were built in 1959, and the first base board, which still supports Ambleden today, was set up after leaving university in 1960. The work has continued without significant interruption ever since.

*A typical Beal picture. Lots of model railway but not much realism—
but how impressive it was. From West Midland, published 1952.*

While all models are built to portray reality, our assessment of the effectiveness of that portrayal depends on our own individual knowledge and experience; it is a subjective judgement. One of the high spots of the Madder Valley when I first encountered it was the trestle bridge carrying the line over the river high up in the hills—a dramatic, exciting, credible, and inspiring piece of landscape modelling. Now, though, a professional lifetime later, and knowing rather more about bridges than I did then, I find the picture is rather less convincing, though I hasten to add that I still regard the model with great affection.

John Ahern's bridge over the River Madder, one of the first attempts to blend the solid foreground into the backscene. But, there was never, ever, a bridge like that. Hugely inspiring nevertheless.

The pictures in this book are of models that are made to look right to me, in the light of my experience. Not for a moment would I suggest that they are 'accurate', as those at Pendon might be considered accurate. My knowledge of thatching, for example, is almost non-existent, limited to what I have picked up from casual observation and photographs. My thatched models look acceptably realistic to me, but I am sure that to an expert thatcher, they would be unconvincing for numerous reasons.

The same applies to the railway. I know little about the technicalities of railways, and have made no attempt to produce precise scale models correct in every detail; indeed, I have neither the knowledge nor the skills to do so. I am quite prepared to accept that the layout of the stations and the trains themselves are 'wrong' in an absolute sense, but they were chosen and built to conjure up the impressions and atmosphere of the railways I once knew as I choose to remember them, as influenced by photographs I have seen and the wrong conclusions I might have reached.

Most model railways are motivated by nostalgia—an attraction for the past as we remember it, or think that we do, or we would like to think that it was. Amberdale is no exception and is strongly influenced by my nostalgic affection for two West Country lines that figured large in my boyhood. Our local line was the branch that left the LSWR main line from Waterloo at Sidmouth Junction and followed the valley of the River Otter southwards to the sea. Through Ottery St Mary to Tipton St Johns, then up the hill to Sidmouth or on down the valley to Newton Poppleford and Budleigh Salterton—there were camping coaches at Newton Poppleford, I remember, or was it at Tipton?

A glimpse of the Madder Valley, by John Ahern. Imaginative modelling that reflects the real world. Published in 1951.

From the bridge at the junction, we would watch long non-descript goods trains rumble past; passenger trains hauled by Bullied Pacifics, the Atlantic Coast Express, the Devon Belle, steaming through on the main line while the branch service waited in the bay platform. Long sunny summer holiday days with bikes, shorts, and sandwiches down the Otter Valley, beside and in the river, looking up as the familiar trains passed by. Rather grubby M7s handled all the traffic, usually just the same couple of green coaches, but occasionally with through coaches to and from Waterloo. We put pennies on the line but were chased off by the nearby crossing keeper. At Ottery, we often had to wait at the level crossing, but it was an exciting excuse to see the railway close up, to watch the signalman exchange the token with the engine crew and actually smell and feel the heat of the huge locomotive as it passed just inches away.

The other railway that so impressed me was the Exe Valley line, which took me to and from school in the 1940s—winding up the valley through the trees, crossing and recrossing the river, and calling at Thorverton, Cadeleigh, West Exe, Tiverton, Cove, and Bampton to the junction at Dulverton, where we changed onto the Taunton to Barnstaple line to continue the journey on to East Anstey. One or two well-worn auto coaches were hauled by a 14XX. The trees did not actually brush the carriage windows, but I like to imagine that they did. To a small boy, it seemed a long journey at the time, but I know now it was only 24 miles and took just over an hour. The number of stations rather than the number of miles colours my memory of the length of the line. Both those lines, now long since closed, are very much a part of Amberdale.

Just as I remember local journeys by train, I also have still earlier memories of riding to school in a trap, the horse walking, never trotting, through the streets of Ottery St Mary. I decided that Amberdale would be set in the 1890s, before the motor car changed everything. It was not, then, so long ago, still within the comfortable memory of many people I knew. Despite accumulating numerous books and photographs of the period my knowledge of it is inevitably limited, so the model represents that time insofar as I like to think it might have been. I know that it includes many anachronisms—a fair number have been pointed out to me—so I claim a little poetic licence from time to time.

When I think back to the railways I knew and loved as a boy, and the circumstances in which I knew them, I am inspired to try to reproduce in model form the impressions that they invoked. What was it that generated my fascination and enthusiasm all those years ago? Whatever it was, that is what I needed to model. I had then no specialised technical knowledge of railways—I still have none—but I have always been captivated by the sight of trains running past, by the excitement of train journeys and the world opened up by a platform ticket. So I have modelled the scene as I like to remember it, innocent of unknown technicalities, my memories made more poignant by replacing taxis with cab horses and motor buses with trams.

This is a very different approach to that taken by many of today's modellers who seek to reproduce the real thing as accurately as possible, whether it be individual models 'correct' to the last rivet or complete stations. I admire hugely the craftsmanship and dedicated research they display, but you will not find evidence of those talents here. Amberdale is, perhaps, a more imaginative, less precise exercise in nostalgia. I hasten to add that such an approach should not be taken as an excuse for lazy modelling; if anything, more care is needed to make an imaginary scene convincing.

Amberdale is built to the popular scale of 4 mm to the foot. A man is about as high as your thumb nail is long. All the models are built from scratch from mundane raw materials such as card, balsa wood, and tinplate and are, with very few exceptions, imaginary. The standard of modelling is not 'state of the art'; I certainly do not claim any particular expertise.

Their construction follows fairly standard procedures, well-known and expertly explained in the many books, magazines, and videos devoted to the subject. As experience and expertise accumulates, one learns tricks of the trade, and skills develop and improve. The work is done more quickly and becomes more effective until things plateau out at an acceptable level compatible with the overall extent of the project and the time available in which to build it. If every model was to be built to Pendon standards, Amberdale would never ever be finished. Pendon, remember, is being built by a large number of people of specialised skills over a period of many years.

Card, paper, watercolour; patience—and imagination. A picture showing the scale size of the model—and a fairly steady hand.

I have learnt that a high level of modelling skill is not nearly as important or effective as simply working to consistent standards, whatever those standards might be, and that the most essential ingredient of all is imagination. As much time has probably been spent dreaming up what to model as actually building the models themselves.

So Amberdale. inspired by my affectionate but hazy memories of the railways I once knew and loved, is an impressionistic model of an imaginary railway set in a continuous and credible landscape, built to standards of accuracy that are acceptable and convincing enough to me to conjure up a little of the atmosphere, wonder and excitement I was lucky enough to enjoy all those years ago. Also, of course, it is a model that has been both fun and challenging to build.

*A typical source of inspiration, from a
postcard painted by A. R. Quinton.*

The Photographs

Just how effective or convincing a model is as a portrayal of reality can only be judged by way of photographs. If the model is in front of you, then the fact that it is a miniature, not the real thing, is inescapable. Yet seen through the lens of a camera from a suitable viewpoint, the actual size is not obvious, and a direct comparison with reality can be made. The pictures in this book seek to portray Amberdale in as convincing a way as possible, to bring the model to life and present it, although it is a fiction, as a real place. The upper photograph shown opposite, a 'realistic' picture of the model shown on page eight, is a view that can only be seen by the camera, it is physically impossible to see it from that angle without doing yourself a serious injury.

On entering the 'railway room', the whole of Amberdale lies before you; its full extent and how it all fits together is immediately revealed.

The photographs in this book, like that on the previous page, not only provide a much better and closer view than is to be had from inspecting the actual model, they also conceal the overall geography of the dale and how each part relates to the others. This element of mystery reflects the intriguing times I had as a boy, trying to piece together the various pictures of the Madder Valley into the whole scene, and may add interest to the following pages.

Here are the towns and villages, the mines and mills, the rivers, roads, and railways of an imagined land. Welcome to Amberdale.

Amberdale

Seen from high above, up there with the seagull, the whole of Amberdale lies before you. It extends, you will remember, from the hills above Hawkridge, where the River Amber rises, as far as the mill town of Wenly, the gateway to the dale. Following the bird as it flies south down the valley, leaving Ambleden behind, a few landmarks will stand out. Hambury Viaduct, carrying the railway high over the river, then the tower of St Michael's Church at Broad Hambury. Just beyond the village the open scar of Oldways Quarry disfigures the landscape, albeit only temporarily, since the workings will have to be made good in due course. Then on down the valley to the steeply wooded banks of the River Sorrel, and the village of Kingslake. The head gear of Kingslake Colliery looms over the small cluster of houses, a foretaste of the mills, chimneys and haze of Wenly, spread out below us at the foot of the dale. While these features all stand out clearly, the keener eyes of a hawk would be needed to pick out the thin line of railway snaking through the valley. All is quiet just now, but one can picture a train 'shoveling white steam over her shoulder' as she labours up the dale to Ambeden.

'Into my heart an air that kills
From yon far country blows.
What are those blue remembered hills,
What spires, what farms, are those?'

'Where the ploughland meets the heather,
And earth from sky divides ...'

The young stream trickles out from under the gorse, splashes down over the rocks and then slows as it widens through the dale. The landscape softens to a more friendly and familiar scene as the curlew are replaced by swans, the heather by willow trees, and the moorland by hedgerows and fields, pulled together by a network of farm tracks and country lanes.

'I come from haunts of coot and her'n,
I make a sudden sally …

… And sparkle out amid the fern
To bicker down a valley.'

'By thirty hills I hurry down,
Or slip between the ridges …

… By forty falls …

… A little town …

… And half a hundred bridges.'

'... And here and there a foamy flake
Upon me as I travel,
With many a silv'ry waterbreak
Above the golden gravel ...'

The distant spires of St David's stand out above the roof tops of Ambleden and across the woods and fields of the dale—sentinel over a landscape of country cottages and corn fields, of stiles and five-bar gates, of farm tracks and leafy lanes—over a somehow familiar reminder of the English countryside.

*'Wherever there's a cottage small,
beside a field of grain …'*

The dale is well worth a closer look. We could hurry through by train or, perhaps, take a little more time over it and 'walk together down an English lane' into the valley to explore.

Who knows—we may even find some lilacs.

Walking is all very well, but it would be a shame to miss the opportunity of joining the family in the passing wagonette as it trots on towards Broad Hambury, our first port of call.

From high up in the wagonette, our first view of Broad Hambury …

… seen from across the fields …

… nestling in the trees.

Broad Hambury

The village of Broad Hambury straddles the lane climbing up the hill to St Michael's Church. Most of the buildings predate the coming of the railway, so are built from local materials found within the range of a horse and cart. With their mossy roofs, ivy-covered walls, and weathered brickwork, they seem as much a part of the natural landscape as the hedgerows and trees that surround them. It is a picture of deep thatch and brightly painted shutters, of hollyhocks and kitchen gardens, of geese, the beck, the weir, and the pub, and of the blacksmith's forge and the village shop, selling everything from boots to herbal remedies. Small boys with jam jars fish for minnows and newts in the village pond, while Cyril fills his water cart before setting off on his rounds. *Sally*, a heavy shire horse, waits patiently outside Mr Reed's bakery while the ploughman collects his lunch, chickens scrabble about in the roadway, and as the church clock strikes twelve, the 'Captain' makes his way slowly up the hill to the White Swan for his daily 'constitutional'.

Ignored by the free-range chickens in the road, the wagonette rumbles into the square. 'Gwens', the village shop, is well-stocked with locally grown fruit and vegetables, although many people grow their own. The 'News' is only on sale because of the forthcoming royal visit; normally, just the local Amberdale Argos is in stock and that is only on Fridays.

Corner Cottage. Honeysuckle tumbles over the porch and a clematis clings to the ivy. Rounding the corner, Auntie Flo is driving a spring cart—a light farm cart that could double up as a trap for local shopping trips.

Mrs Hill is calling young Alfie in for his tea. He is coming just as fast as his hoop will carry him.

Rose Cottage—bath night. Annie is carrying the water in from the well using a yoke across her shoulders. It will be heated up on the fire, then poured into the tin bath presently hanging on the wall of the lean-to. After the family have bathed in turn and if there has not been much recent rain, the water might be emptied onto the kitchen garden. Water was precious and used sparingly.

The Bakery, the premises of Mr Reed, the village baker—maker of exceedingly fine cakes. Sammy Luxton, the local carter, leads Sonia down the hill to deliver a new rolled-up carpet to the vicarage.

Pushing out the envelope—there is a new building on the edge of the village, made by local tradesmen with locally sourced materials. The thatch was often unlined, with the residents sleeping under the straw.

Until the Second World War, milking was generally done in the open fields. Most was shipped out to the towns by train, but local deliveries were made from a churn in the back of a milk float, a ladleful at a time into the housewife's jug.

Cottage Gardens

Colourful flower gardens are felt to be an essential ingredient of the village scene, though they were in fact a rare luxury not many could afford. The land could be better used, and few had the leisure time to cultivate them, but they are attractive.

The greenhouse was the first object in the dale to be bought by mail order; the tomatoes are coming on lovely.

'Just now the lilac is in bloom …   *All before my little room,*

And in my flowerbeds, I think,
Smile the carnation and the pink;

And down the borders, well I know,
The poppy and the pansy blow …'

The flower garden was very much the icing on the cake; it was the kitchen garden that really mattered. Here are grown cabbages, marrows, carrots, potatoes, and something that looks rather like rhubarb, but one cannot be sure.

And, of course, the most important business of all—keeping a pig. They would be shared out between the neighbours—you could eat everything except the squeak. This is Bunter, an English Saddleback.

Wander up the busy main street to the spiritual centre of the village—the White Swan, the church, and the village pond. The latter was an important asset to the community, often sited in the void left after digging out the materials used to build the houses. Here, though, it was made by building a weir across Hambury Beck. The pond was essential for fire-fighting—all that thatch about—watering livestock through the summer and, by way of Cyril and his water cart, for domestic supplies to those without a well.

Hambury Beck tumbles down from the hills into the village, splashes over the weir and runs on down the valley to join the Amber.

The pub, the pond, the water cart, the bridge over the weir, an elegant carriage, some white ducks, and Sally ambling past on her way to home farm. Broad Hambury in the sunshine of a summer morning.

The replaced dormer window is indicative of the coming of the railway and the availability of new materials.

The White Swan. The countryside was far quieter than we are used to today. You would have heard the scratching chickens or the crunch of carriage wheels on the gravel at any time of the day. The chimes of the church clock could be heard on the hour anywhere in the village.

A closer look at the governess cart.

Honeysuckle cottage, with Gran'ma baby-sitting. The pram was probably bought third or fourth hand at jumble sale held in the village hall.

The forge is sited beside the pond because Stan needs water to quench the hot ironwork.

Stan Tweddle is the blacksmith. He made and mended both farm machinery and domestic tools, and was by tradition the village barber. He rolls his sleeves inwards so that sparks do not get trapped in the turn-ups.

The lychgate outside St Michael's Church. It was here, not, as you may have been taught, at Stoke Poges, that Gray was inspired to compose his 'Elegy in a Country Churchyard'. Many of us remember at least the first verse.

'The curfew tolls the knell of parting day,

The lowing herd winds slowly o'er the lea,

The ploughman homeward plods his weary way,

And leaves the world to darkness and to me.'

Our cue to be moving on.

Broad Hambury Station

The railway runs through Broad Hambury in a cutting, so the trains themselves cannot be seen from the village nor the village from the train. As we approach the station, the trees crowd in over the carriages, and drifting steam spoils the view through the windows. The wheel beat slows as the train rounds the curve, and, with a squeal of brakes, pulls up alongside a milk train standing in the down platform. Although a very small station, it is nevertheless quite an important one. The branch line to the Endovers joins the main line here, and a loop line enables up and down trains to pass each other—last in, first out. The small goods yard is a regular port of call for the daily pick-up goods that runs up the valley from Wenly.

The southern approach to Broad Hambury station. The cattle pens and the coal office are on the right, and the jib of the 5-ton crane points into the sky. The Endover branch comes in on the left just in front of the signal box. An up train waits for an approaching milk train to clear the line—and leave the station—before running on down to Kingslake.

A dog cart waits outside the ticket office—if closed, try the shop opposite. To catch the train, go over the footbridge and down to the platform. Lit by oil lamps, the guard of the last train through in the evening turns them out as he leaves.

The view from the bridge during rush hour at Broad Hambury station.

Oldways Quarry

Oldways Quarry figured large in the prospectus drawn up for the construction of the line in 1868. It was seen as an important source of traffic and has not disappointed. Stone blasted from the quarry face is hauled down to the crushing plant in horse-drawn skips, running through the quarry on a roughly laid narrow-gauge railway. The skips are tipped into a receiving hopper, from which a steam-powered bucket conveyor lifts the stone to the top of the building for crushing and screening before being let down into railway wagons for dispatch. All the buildings are, of course, temporary, built from corrugated iron sheeting. They will be removed when the workings are exhausted.

Oldways Quarry, seen from across the fields near Broad Hambury.

Quarried stone is led down to the workings in horse-drawn skips …

… where they are tipped into a hopper.

Daisy *arrives with a train of empty wagons. She will drop the brake van off at the station before backing the train under the screens for loading.*

The workings. On the right is the receiving hopper, in front of which is the engine house, with the conveyor rising up behind it. The current quarry face is to the left, behind the screening building.

Daisy *sets off with a fully loaded train. It is a steep bank down the line, so strict regulations apply—no more than five loaded wagons at a time, and the brakes pinned down.*

Hambury Viaduct

Hambury Viaduct carries the railway high above the floodplain of the River Amber. It is the most—indeed, the only—significant piece of engineering on what is otherwise an unassuming little railway. Viaducts of this type were designed by Brunel for his lines in the West Country. They were cheap to build but high on maintenance, a lack of lateral strength being the main problem. The last of the type was replaced in the 1930s. Hambury was built—without scaffolding, as was then the way—in 1873, rather later than those in other parts of the country and is standing up to traffic quite well after some twenty years of service.

It is hard today to appreciate the impact that the appearance of structures like this had on country people. They had not been forewarned by experience or photography and would gaze up in disbelief at trains running through the sky. It was as near to flying as you could imagine.

The gig with the red wheels is a Whisky, the 'sports car' of its day.

Preserved locomotive Hazel *crosses the viaduct with
an enthusiasts' special late on a summer evening.*

*One reads of structures like this 'striding across the landscape'.
They really do. Far below is the roof of Winsford Mill.*

Winsford Mill

Walking out onto the high girders and into the wind, we can look down to the river far below and onto the roof of Winsford Mill. The watermill and the windmill were the only practical alternatives to steam power, though their use was limited because they could only be sited in those locations where wind and water conditions were suitable, not necessarily where the power might actually be needed. Winsford mill predates the railway by some 100 years and was worked until the middle of the twentieth century.

A weir is built across the stream to develop the head or drop in water level, needed to power the wheel and to store water in a headpond or reservoir.

Paddles in the mill control the flow of water from the headpond into the head race, the water channel leading to the wheel.

The head race, accelerating the water onto the wheel. The footbridge gives access to the outer bearing of the wheel.

*The wheel also powers the sack hoist by way of shafting
carried through the roof of the building.*

*Splashing off the wheel, the water cascades
down the tail race into the River Amber.*

The mill wheel turns two pairs of grinding stones and drives the sack hoist. The stones are imported from France, a particularly hard type of granite found near Paris. After turning the wheel, the water falls away down the tail race. This further drop in water level protects the wheel from flooding, which might otherwise put it out of use. The head pond and the tail race enable the mill to continue working irrespective of the flow in the river. The River Win tumbles into the Amber just upstream of the fourteenth-century pack horse bridge.

This is a breast-shot wheel, the water hitting the paddles at 2 o'clock and splashing off at about 7. It rotates clockwise at 8 rpm.

Along the Valley Road

The main effect the coming of the railways had on local traffic was to increase it as increasing prosperity and the railways generated more movement of people and goods. This encouraged an improvement in the road surfaces, but out in the country, they remained a hazard. The options remained a choice between walking, riding, or, if affordable, a horse-drawn carriage—and what a variety there was.

Most were designed empirically and built by local coach builders and wheel wrights, whose aim was to keep the weight to a minimum, maximizing the load that the horse could pull. At the same time, they had to be strong enough to survive the punishing road surface, and there had to be a compromise between larger wheels for easier pulling and smaller for better manoeuvrability. The earlier vehicles, built with a perch or chassis, gave way to lighter carriages with the body mounted on leaf springs attached directly to the under gear. Until the turn of the century, most commercial vehicles were led; reins only became compulsory after that date. Heavy horse-drawn wagons remained in use well into the 1950s, and most of the traffic over Tower Bridge was horse-drawn until 1946.

'Walk on'. A bow top gypsy caravan ambles past Hambury Viaduct on the valley road. The roof, built up from ledges on each side of the bodywork, is covered in canvas lined with carpet and makes a snug home for the family. The van is pulled by Jesse, the traditional painted horse, along a lane lined with poppies and dandelions.

Geese to market. Their feet were dipped in tar and sprinkled with sand to protect them from the road.

An Oxfordshire or Woodstock wagon harnessed to a pair of shorthorn oxen by a yoke or oxbow. It was a common sight until the 1920s.

The 1890s was the heyday of the bicycle. More than 1 million were being made each year. The 'Ordinary'—or penny farthing—was being replaced by the modern safety bicycle.

Trump's deliver groceries round the dale.
What elegant vehicles they were.

A two-seat buggy, with a
dicky seat for the groom.

A Victoria.

What was it like?

*'You could sit behind a team of
snow-white horses in the slickest
rig you would ever see …*

*Well, one's like snow,
the other's more like milk'.*

*'Chicks and ducks and geese better
scurry, when I take you out in the
Surrey, when I take you out in the
Surrey with the fringe on top.'*

'Riding slowly home in the Surrey'.

This graceful owner-driven carriage, copied from a painting by Stubbs, was probably built about the end of the eighteenth century, but it was kept in use until the end of the nineteenth. The body is suspended from the wooden under gear on leather straps. The perch is shaped to improve the full lock of the front wheels. The matched pair of horses are wearing breast harnesses, which predated the introduction of the collar, but continued in widespread use, particularly by the military because, unlike the collar, it would fit any horse.

The impressive hat would, surely, have been firmly secured with a substantial hat pin.

The post-chaise was the first carriage to use steel springs—called 'C' springs, though the body was still hung from them on leather straps. These evolved into the semi and then the fully elliptical leaf springs still used today, seen here on this canoe landau.

On the Land

In the 1890s, the farmers of Amberdale were still entirely dependent on horses to work the land as steam ploughing had not yet reached into the dale. Nevertheless, increasing use is being made of machinery, both in the fields and about the farm. The number of people working on the land has fallen hugely over the last few decades, many moving into the towns to feed industrial mechanization in mills and factories.

Springfield, Frank Potter's farm at Daisy Mount, is typical of those lower down the dale. Cows, heavy horses, chickens, geese, pigeons, hay, mud and wonderful farmyard smells.

Springfield Farm, Daisy Mount.

Frank and Bessie Potter.

Frank's wife Bessie arrives back at the farm after delivering some eggs to the village shop.

The original farmhouse has been extended to enlarge the kitchen and add a small dairy. Free-range egg production is in progress.

The threshing barn. The outside stairway is quite a common feature, built thus to save space inside the building.

Romantic maybe, but hard and lonely work. Horses required a lot of attention. The horseman would often start work at four or five in the morning, feeding, rubbing down, and harnessing up in preparation for the day's work; they were often the last to finish at night when the horses were finally bedded down.

'Where the ploughland meets the heather …'
High above Hawkridge, where the river rises.

Queenie *ploughing near Home Farm.*
The iron plough was introduced in the
1860s, the seagulls rather earlier.

The sail reaper was a second-generation harvesting machine, not only cutting the corn—replacing the scything gangs—but also sweeping it to one side to leave a clear path for the horses the next time around. The cut corn is gathered into sheaves that are then stooked to dry out in the sun.

A sail reaper, pulled by two mid-weight horses.

Leading the harvest home, in this case a load of hay. Working horses were almost invariably led.

Hay ride.

The harvest was brought back and stacked in the rick yard, immediately adjacent to the farm yard. The stacks were built on assorted pieces of wood to raise them clear of the ground, to keep them dry and hopefully as a precaution against rats, but also offering some protection to poultry. The ricks were tightly thatched against winter storms, remaining a common and welcome sight in the countryside well into the twentieth century.

The rick yard at Springfield farm.

High summer in Amberdale, as we like to remember it.

The corn was threshed over the winter in the threshing barn. Manual threshing, using flails, was gradually superseded by mechanisation from the beginning of the nineteenth century, and Springfield is now typical of its time.

A horse gin—or one horse power engine house—is attached to the barn and drives the threshing machine inside by way of gearing and shafting from the centre post pushed around by the horse. The large barn doors at the front and shutters at the back of the building would be opened, enabling a through draft to blow away the chaff.

The horse gin, or gin-gang, at Springfield farm. Apparently quite popular with the horses, the unattended animal was left to plod round the well-worn track, turning the vertical shaft and the gearing attached thereto, driving the machine in the adjacent barn. Many such buildings remained in use until the 1950s, and though the machinery has long gone, many still stand.

Racing the storm.

In Amberdale, the sun shines—well, most of the time. The harvesters picnic their lunch in the fields while the big horses munch through their nose bags and rabbits take the opportunity to run out of the corn. During the long summer days of harvesting, the farmyard itself is quiet but for the scratching of chickens and cooing of pigeons—and the sound of Bessie, preparing the evening meal.

Out in the fields at harvest time, it was a very, very long day, from dawn till dusk.

The Coming of the Railway

The 1890s were the heyday of the railways. They were the wonder of the age, extending to every corner of the land. Few places were not within walking distance of a railway station. After the trunk lines had been built, branch lines were pushed out into the more remote countryside, transforming the lives of the people who lived there. One such line was built to wind its way through the buttercup fields of Amberdale, up the valley to Ambleden.

The East Coast Railway, which runs through the valley, was built in the 1870s and opened to Ambleden on 18 April 1875. Perhaps the promoters hoped that the line would eventually extend to the east coast, though in the event it never did. The railway opened up the dale to the outside world as well as the outside world to Amberdale. The most significant and immediate changes were the reduction in the cost of coal and the practicality of travel out of the dale. Most people had previously never left the district in which they were born.

Changing times. The mail coach that used to ply between Wenly and Ambleden is falling apart, pigeons are nesting in the bodywork, and a wheel has been salvaged to repair a farm cart. The sound of the post horn has long been replaced by the train whistle.

… through buttercup fields …

Posters, preaching as ever to the converted, extol the delights of train travel and services through the dale.

Coal—1,000 tons at a time, to anywhere in the country, replacing the two or three tons delivered by a heavy horse-drawn wagon.

SEE BRITAIN BY TRAIN
AMBERDALE
THROUGH AND LOCAL SERVICES
APPLY TO YOUR LOCAL STATION
EAST COAST RAILWAY

EXPRESS PARCELS
SERVING ANYWHERE IN
AMBERDALE
CONTACT YOUR LOCAL PARCEL OFFICE
WENLY AMBLEDEN BROAD HAMBURY
KINGSLAKE CHUTNEY ENDOVERS
EAST COAST RAILWAY

Our wagonette has given way to trains travelling at a mile a minute, right out of the dale to the wide world beyond.

The oldest bit of 'railwayana' to be found in the dale is *Rowena*. She was built by Robert Stephenson in 1827, between *Locomotion No. 1* and the *Rocket* and continues to work at Kingslake Colliery, a working life of some seventy years, matching that of *Puffing Billy*. Fitted with a return flue boiler, the fireman works at the front, leaving the driver alone on the footplate. She has been recorded (unofficially) of reaching a speed of 17 mph—unloaded, of course.

Rowena, *1827 to date.*

Another fine old locomotive is Hazel. *Bought second-hand by the contractor, she was used during the construction of the line.*

Following parliamentary approval, construction of the line began in 1872 and was finally completed three years later. The extensive cuttings near Broad Hambury and Hambury Viaduct took longer and cost more than anticipated, but such overruns were the normal way of things. The raw earthworks have long since grown back into the countryside; the railway is now lost in the landscape.

To mark the completion of the line, Hazel *was sold to the company and formally named by Lady Hazel on 29 February 1875. She—that is, the locomotive—had the honour of hauling the first scheduled service on the occasion of the grand opening on 18 April 1875.*

Billy Darkings and his gang of navvies working near Broad Hambury, 3 September 1874.
Hazel, *then unnamed, is prominent in the background.*

Rowena *working at Kingslake Colliery, c. 1880.*

The branch to the Endovers was built in the 1880s. The locomotive *Sam* was used by the contractor and, again, on completion of the works, passed into the ownership of the company.

Sam *during construction at Endover High,*
the terminus of the branch.

Whuen the line to the Endovers was opened, passenger services were limited to just *Sam* and her combined saloon/baggage car. Each was fitted with a 'cow-catcher' or pilot because Lord McElhinney would not allow fences to be built across his deer park. His decision was subsequently reversed in light of the number of deer fatalities, but the cow-catchers have yet to be removed.

In the early days there were no run-round facilities at Endover High, so *Sam* pushed the coach back on the return trip. Since 1889, when a run-round loop was built, the service has been taken over by *Harriet* and her train of 'proper' coaches; *Sam* only appears on special occasions.

Sam leaving the Endover branch and entering Broad Hambury station.

On the return trip from Ambleden, the baggage car leads, here approaching Hambury Viaduct.

On one memorable occasion, a local farmer decided that 'baggage', as in 'baggage car', could well include pigs—or at least a pig. With no written regulations to contradict his assertion, the reluctant animal was duly despatched to be off-loaded at Broad Hambury. How the fare was calculated, or by whom, has not been recorded.

Needless to say, the unfortunate animal escaped and trapped its head in the timber work under the platform, causing much excitement and a serious delay to following trains.

The matter was eventually sorted, and both the trains and the pig were able to continue on their way. However, the railway company introduced permanent changes to their operating procedures.

We got the message—no more pigs.

EAST COAST RAILWAY

NOTICE

THE CARRIAGE OF LIVESTOCK IN PASSENGER CARRYING VEHICLES IS PROHIBITED, WITH THE EXCEPTION OF DOGS, CAGED BIRDS, AND WHITE MICE [WHICH MUST BE SECURELY BOXED].

PENALTY 40/-

BY ORDER

7 JULY 1889

The Railway Today

Now twenty years since it was opened, the railway has settled into its natural place in the landscape. The service ran virtually unchanged for some ninety years, until finally closed by Dr Beeching in the 1960s. You could set your watch by the plume of steam rising above the hedgerows as the familiar trains ran past—'give or take half an hour or so'. The train crews became well-known to the farmers and cottagers along the line and would often stop to drop off or collect a parcel or some rabbits, even, let it be said, in the winter the odd shovel of coal. The railway was very much part of the rural community it served—much loved and valued by all.

Chloe, with the Chutney railcar, drifts down the bank to join the main line just south of Wenly station. While travelling in this direction, the driver joins the fireman on the footplate. For the return journey, he controls the engine from the far end of the trailer. As railcars were kept in engine sheds, they tended to be rather mucky.

Onich, *with mixed goods, approaching a cattle crossing, deep in the countryside.*

Harriet *heads for the hills.*

Arrival into Broad Hambury. The solitary cattle van is indicative of how important the cattle traffic was. Prior to the railways, beasts were moved on the hoof, which resulted in a significant loss of weight and hence value. Bringing them into town by train made an enormous difference.

The pride of the line—the *Amber Arrow* Pullman service that runs through the dale on Saturday afternoons in the summer. The elegant single-driver locomotive has been withdrawn from full-time service and now only runs with the *Arrow*. She glides along at about 40 mph, affording plenty of time to admire the view.

Travel by Pullman has always been a privilege thanks to the polished woodwork, the deeply upholstered cushions, the white table cloths and table lamps, the white coated waiters, and the smoothness of the ride. Tea is served at your seat while the countryside slides by the window.

The observation car is rather special—watching the track unfold behind the train, people waving from the lineside, passing stations receding into the distance to disappear round the bend, signals returning to 'danger' as we pass.

Afternoon tea, at your seat. The first sitting was immediately after leaving Wenly on the outward journey, the second on leaving Ambleden on the return.

The Arrow, *waved through by the signalman, glides through Kingslake station.*

The menu. It did not change much, if at all, but was always just right for the occasion.

Tea is also served, at your seat, in the observation car. The excitement never faded.

From Broad Hambury, on down the line to Kingslake, our next port of call. If your journey had started at the Endovers, you would have to change trains at Broad Hambury to join the main line train running through to Wenly. This could involve quite a long wait on the rather draughty platform—pleasant in the summer, but not so much fun in the winter. If you were lucky, the signalman might invite you in for a cuppa and a warm up by his fire; it very much depended on the mood he was in at the time. A gratuity at Christmas would not go amiss.

Onich ready to depart from Broad Hambury. At the appointed time, the signal drops, doors are slammed shut, whistles are exchanged between the guard and the driver, and the train moves slowly forward.

The train would bounce along at about 25 miles per hour. The speed was determined by the comfort tolerance of the passengers as much as anything else.

Her train crosses the River Sorrel, a tributary of the Amber, which it joins at Watersmeet, about half a mile downstream of the bridge.

Approaching Kingslake, crossing the Sorrel bridge.

Coasting into Kingslake station. The level crossing gates protect the narrow-gauge line where it crosses the main line just outside the station.

Met by a solitary porter, though probably sufficient for the number of passengers—two or three at the most.

Kingslake

Waiting for a train on Kingslake's solitary platform, you would often hear it chuffing through the valley towards you from the moment it left the previous station. The countryside was far quieter then, and even when the train was standing in the station, one could still hear the sound of birdsong and the waterfalls just beyond the of the platform. Remote country stations like Kingslake were possibly best described by Edward Thomas in his recollection of Adlestrop—or was it Kingslake?

'The steam hissed, someone cleared his throat,
No-one left and no-one came.
On the bare platform what I saw
Was Kingslake, only the name.

And willows, willow herb and grass,
And meadow-sweet and haycocks dry,
No whit less still and lonely fair
Than the high cloudlets in the sky.

And for that minute a blackbird sang,
Close by, and round him, mistier,
Farther and farther, all the birds
Of Amberdale, across the Shire.'

It was, quite literally, a quiet life in a station like this. A few local farmers used the station to ship out vegetables and milk, and there was a fair amount of cattle traffic, but most trains ran through without stopping. The facilities are minimal—a covered shelter for the few passengers and a small goods shed that is little more than a parcels office, which also serves as a mess room for the two permanent staff. They are usually pleased to see you and will often invite you in for a cup of tea and one of Mr Reed's cakes—it breaks up what otherwise might be a rather monotonous day.

Of course, one could not sit drinking tea all day as the cattle pens have to be cleaned out now and then. An unpopular duty, they take it in turns. Watching the other fellow do it is some measure of compensation.

A moment of high drama, some sheep—Amberdales probably—have come down from the hills and are trying to invade the office …

… and stray onto the platform. Once they are cleared away, or at least have settled down, we can make our way into the village.

Old cottages beside the Sorrel, built safely above river level in
light of the catastrophic floods back in 1705. Some roof repairs are
outstanding, but only the geese are shut in there at night.

The Diggers Rest, the village pub. Posed in the doorway is the pub cat, Sukie, and on the extreme right the gateway into Kingslake Colliery. The pub was a popular stopping-off point for miners coming off their shift, though the practice was frowned on by the management.

Terraces near the colliery and a glimpse into their backyards. The tinker's cart contains a fine old iron bedstead, recovered from a local pond.

The outside privy and the tame rabbit.

The scrubbing board and the mangle make wash day almost a pleasure.

L ooming over the roof tops, the head gear of the colliery dominates the village. Kingslake Colliery is typical of the small privately owned mines spread across the English coal fields between about 1800 and 1950.

Kingslake Colliery

The railways were originally developed and built specifically to transport coal, and coal remained their principal business until the end of the twentieth century. Before the railway through Amberdale was built, the mine at Kingslake was very small, supplying coal by horse wagons to nearby Wenly. Development of the mine figured largely in the prospectus for the proposed railway, and it duly expanded to supply a far wider market. It is now an important source of traffic, shipping coal out through Wenly to the wider world beyond, and supplying local coal merchants for deliveries through the dale.

Mine pumping and coal winding drove the development of the steam engine. The first atmospheric engine pump invented by Newcomen was developed by James Watt into the pressure-driven, double-acting steam engine that effectively fired the industrial revolution. George Stephenson and his contemporaries adapted Watt's static engine to run on rails, replacing the tall furnace chimney with the blast pipe and refining the design of the rail and the flanged wheel.

The boiler house. The two Lancashire boilers generate steam to drive the winding engine that lifts the coal to the surface. Pit props are stacked ready for use underground. The wooden head gear was replaced by a steel structure shortly after this picture was taken.

The pipe bridge carries steam out to the engine house, then the condensate back to the boiler.

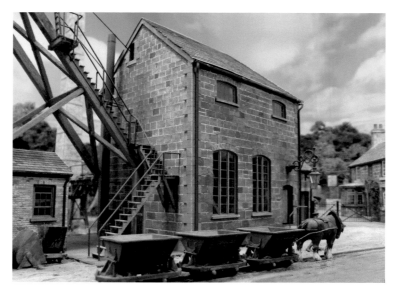

The engine or winding house.

The Crowther type of winding engine in the engine house. The stairs give access to the upper gallery.

The winding drum, the flywheel, and the associated brake gear. An indicator mechanism is attached to the drum, so that the engine-man can control the cages, or lifts, as they move up and down the shaft.

The head gear stands between the engine house and the screening building, The loaded skips are manhandled from the cage and weighed, then tipped onto the screening bars to be discharged into waiting railway wagons. The entire mining process, from hewing at the coalface to loading wagons for dispatch, depended on hard manual labour in harsh conditions, and an awful lot was needed. Coal was the lifeblood of the country. The demand—from battleships to railways, from industry to domestic hearths—was insatiable.

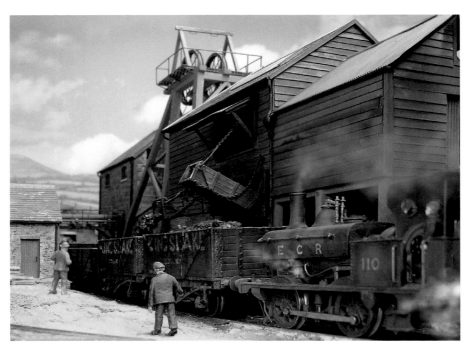

The railway doing what it was built to do. Several hundred tons of hard-won coal pulls out of the colliery on its way out of the dale. The heavily loaded loose-coupled wagons are unbraked, with the safety of the train depending on the brake van and the locomotive.

Waste spoil was brought up with the coal and had to be disposed of. A narrow-gauge railway serves this purpose, running from the colliery up the valley of the Sorrel to a suitable site hidden in the trees. This view of the line winding between the buildings, the empty hopper rusting in the sunshine, is iconic.

Local deliveries, by a pair of heavy horses in tandem, pulling a coal chariot, a purpose-built heavy wagon. Weighing scales are stowed under the tail board.

Rowena, *now some seventy years old, continues to work at the colliery. She leads coal from the screens to the boiler house.*

The narrow-gauge track crosses the main line just outside Kingslake station, under the immediate and watchful eye of the signalman. It runs under the trees and tight to the water's edge, the beat of the exhaust frightening the kingfishers and the occasional heron. The trees really do brush the passing trains.

The locomotive, *Lynn*, is based on the familiar Darjeeling type still in use in India. Unlike her Indian relatives, who each require a crew of five, she manages under the sole control of driver, Hull, and his fireman, George.

Wenly

The mill town of Wenly stands as the gateway to Amberdale. The oldest part of the town is clustered around St Peter's Church—cobbled streets and alleyways, timber-framed buildings jettied out over the lower floors, small workshops, outside stairways, weaver's garrets, washing strung between the upper windows, and poky little corner shops. The narrow streets are cluttered with horse-drawn carts, carriages, and vans of every sort, with Hansom cabs, horse buses, and now trams that rattle and whine as they grind up Bank Street to the station. The huge cotton mills, which now dominate the skyline, were built back in the 1860s and 1870s, and their chimneys now cast their shadows over rows of back-to-back terraced housing, stretching out into the suburbs along the extending tram lines.

Street scenes around Wenly—the indispensable corner shop; the mid-Victorian pub; the jobbing builder; the clean washing hung out, optimistically, to dry; the factory clock; the tram lines climbing the bank; and the horse bus trying to avoid them.

These mill buildings were the first to be built to mathematical design and engineering drawings. Far from being 'dark and satanic', they were light and airy by the standards of the day—conditions essential for the operation of the spinning frames and other machinery within. The risk of fire was the main hazard.

The huge smoking chimneys were not an eyesore but a welcome sight as they signified employment.

A rear view of Nos 435 to 457, Mill Terrace, Wenly.

As the mills went up, miles (literally) of terrace housing were built in their shadow to accommodate the work force. They had to live within walking distance of the mill since there was no affordable public transport at that time. It was the coming of the electric tramways in the 1880s, which drove the expansion of the towns out into the suburbs.

Amber Mills. Steam-powered by a triple-expansion engine, the sophisticated descendant of the primitive winding engine at the colliery. The building would contain carding machines, spinning frames, and looms—the whole process.

Compared to today, and except on high days and holidays, the streets were practically deserted. What traffic there was was almost entirely commercial.

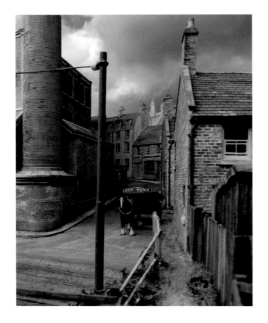

A Hansom, as updated by Joseph Chapman.

The Wenly Co-op was opened in 1867.

A pantechnicon, Wenly and the World.

A heavy railway delivery van.

Ringtons Tea.

Door-to-door deliveries.

Road-to-rail container traffic.

*Cotton bales going
into Amber Mills.*

A 'Camel-top' baker's van.

A Brougham carriage, for hire.

An early private horse bus, scheduled to follow a specified route and timetable.

The early 'Knife board' bus, with footboards, evolved into the 'Garden Seat' bus, the footboards into the decency board, designed to encourage ladies onto the upper deck.

The two-horse bus required a team of up to twelve horses to maintain a full day service, and the working life of the animals was very limited. This burden was reflected in the high fares, which in turn limited their appeal to the general public. It was the coming of the electric tramways—which in turn had evolved from horse-drawn trams—that first brought public transport within the reach of working people. The tram lines soon pushed out into the suburbs, and the towns quickly expanded, absorbing nearby villages and countryside.

The Wenly Electric Traction Company (WETC) opened their first line, between the station and the terminus at Amber Mills, in 1889. Their open-top cars are similar to those working on the Bristol tramway, though finished in the smart livery of the WETC. Bouncing down Wenly Bank on the upper deck in the sunshine can be quite—indeed, very—exhilarating. It is not much fun going up the hill in the rain, though, when the car is full.

Car No. 9 heads out into the suburbs.

On to Wenly station—by cab if you could afford it, by tram if you could not.

The decency board advertises the local paper …

… and here it is, actually being read.

Wenly Station

Wenly station reflects the optimism of the company when the railway was built, and its continuing importance as the traffic hub of Amberdale. Train journeys through the dale start and finish here, from the early—very early—indeed, overnight—milk train to the daily pick-up goods and to the glamour of the *Amber Arrow*. The station never sleeps.

The station building is supported on steel girders spanning the tracks and platforms, a ploy to offset the high cost of land in built up areas.

Who has not waited on draughty platforms like these? This is platform 1, arrival from the dale and departure point to the world beyond.

The atmosphere and excitement of an important station in the 1890s was entrancing. Here is where things happen. The whine of passing tramcars merges with the clatter of horses' hooves and carriage wheels, mixing with the whistles and exhausts of the trains, the shouts of porters, the sound of slamming doors, the smell of the smoke, the steam, and the refreshment room.

EAST COAST RAILWAY
WENLY REFRESHMENT ROOM

Menu Selection

Bread, butter & ~~jam~~ OFF

Currant bun

~~cup~~ of tea

REFRESH YOURSELF BEFORE , DURING
AND AFTER YOUR JOURNEY.

TRAVEL BY TRAIN

'Stands the clock at ten to three?
And are refreshments still for tea?'

Wenly South Yard. The milk bay spans the track in the middle distance.
The churns, more than 300 on most days, are raised to street level by a hydraulic lift.

A far cry from the rural idyll of Broad Hambury—not many blackbirds here.

… a hive of activity.

The goods and grain warehouse …

Two views of the lifting gantry that dominates the south yard. The girders are really far too heavy for the capacity of the lifting tackle but were salvaged from 'elsewhere'.

Wenly South Box. This box controls the southern approaches to the station and the south yard. Casual visitors are NOT welcome, and a Christmas gratuity will not help much either.

ON SHED AT WENLY MPD

The Old Lady *emerges from Victoria Works after some heavy maintenance.*

Daisy *on the turntable. Tank engines were turned from time to time, apparently to even out tyre wear.*

The engine sheds, framed between Katherine, *the chief engineer's saloon, and* Emily, *the Forney type, whose acquisition by the company remains something of a mystery.*

After a wash and brush up, Precedent-class Caroline emerges from the sheds and runs light engine into platform 1 to pick up her waiting train. On the stroke of twelve, she departs with the midday nonstop to Ambleden—making rather too much fuss. She will probably have to replace the Old Lady in Victoria Works for some major attention in the very near future.

The 12.15 All Stations to Ambleden (Wk Days Only)

Adams Radial *Helen* pulls away from Wenly with the 12.15 for Ambleden. Ideally suited to the sharp curves and stiff gradients of the line, she works the day-to-day shuttle service through the dale.

A sunny day, a clear road, and the engine is steaming well. What more could a driver ask? 'God's in his heaven, all's right with the world'.

Passing the colliery on the right. On the left, Chloe descending the bank from Chutney with the railcar before coasting into the bay platform at Wenly.

A last look back at Wenly. The allotment is worked by one of the signalmen. Of course, there is always someone who can tell you how to do it better.

And so, out into the country.

BUT THEN

Cows on the line!

A conference between
the driver and the guard.
Whose turn is it this time?

The guard's. He sets off to find the farmer.

It is quite a walk.

Meanwhile, the situation starts to deteriorate …

… and continues to do so. We are obviously here for the duration.

Some passengers decided it would be quicker to walk.

But eventually, the farmer was found, and he promised to send Alice along 'If I can find her, you know what she's like'.

Finally found, Alice, who is not to be hurried, drives the animals to where they can stand to one side, allowing the train to continue its journey. The incident has delayed the train by nearly an hour.

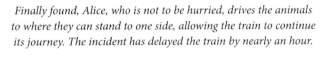

A cheerful wave from the guard— this might mean a bit of overtime.

The train finally arrives in Broad Hambury over an hour late, to be met by an irate Mrs Dowson who vents her fury on the unfortunate guard. 'It's just not good enough—I've a mind to tell my sister, who is married to the station master at Wenly, and he is very important'. After a further fifteen minutes of trying, unsuccessfully, to console her, the train continues on its way.

Mother says 'Don't get smuts in your eye'.

'There is the mill, and here is the river.

Each a glimpse, then gone for ever.'

On, over the canal and the level crossing. Climbing up on the gate—provided the signalman does not warn you off—the huge locomotive passes just inches away, close enough to feel the heat and smell the smell.

The short journey from Broad Hambury to Ambleden does not afford much opportunity for the driver to recover lost time, and the permanent speed limit on the line is not much help either. Experienced passengers resign themselves to the delay and make the most of the passing scenery. The view from the viaduct never fails to provoke wonder.

Journey's end.

And so into Ambleden station some eighty minutes late, it is true, but it is a lovely day and there are not that many passengers anyway, so who is counting?

Ambleden Station

Ambleden station is our destination, the end of the line. Small and apparently insignificant though it might appear, by the complexities of tracks and timetables, it is nevertheless a part of the national railway system, no less an important part than any other. It is connected directly to long coal trains winding through the Welsh valleys, to diminutive far-away trains lost in the immensity of the Forth Bridge, to commuter trains fussing around the capital. Ambleden is on the map.

The railway has rightly been called 'the great connector'. The line of rails stretching away from the end of the platforms leads, quite literally, to anywhere in the world. Stations like this have been, and will be, witness to great events—family gatherings for weddings and funerals, tearful goodbyes to soldiers off to war, and emotional reunions with those who return. Bunting comes out for visiting dignitaries, crepe paper for the death of a queen. Events punctuate the day-to-day routine of a rural community whose way of life has become dependent upon it and which, by its coming, has been changed for ever.

Walk up the platform, bounded by the familiar white paling fence, lined with oil lamps, honeysuckle, and enamel advertisements—VIROL -SUNSHINE SOAP—past the churns and assorted barrows, the pigeon baskets and the luggage-going PLA, to the porter's room, and the ticket and parcels office. Fires burn year-round, and faded posters advertise the delights of railway travel in Amberdale.

Outside the station gate, a Brougham and a Clarence wait for fares, their horses motionless, heads down, as the drivers lean on the fence and agree the life isn't what it was. On past the lamp store (strictly no admittance, by order) and the footbridge to the far end of the platform is the working end. There are water cranes here, where arriving locomotives take water, the fireman clambering up onto the tank or tender top with the canvas trunking while the more sedate driver opens the valve on the platform. In winter, fires are lit beside the cranes to stop them freezing. and the ramps can be slippery with ice, but in summer, any spillage dries quickly, washing away the dust where the sparrows play.

Built on the outskirts of town, that did not remain the case for long, as new buildings clustered around the railway.

The footbridge to platform 2, a classic example of railway architecture. There is not much protection from the elements, maybe, but it affords a grandstand view of the station.

The small locomotive shed at the end of the platforms is home to the engines working the Endover branch; main line engines are serviced at Wenly. The bay window lights the foreman's office, wherein he sorts out shift rotas, servicing schedules, stores, and all the other voluminous paperwork needed to run a railway, even a very small one.

The country station as one remembers it—misty sunshine, the view along the length of the platforms to the turntable in the far distance, simmering in the haze, and a small tank locomotive with a wisp of steam curling up from the chimney as it waits patiently to depart for who knows where.

There are occasional voices, perhaps the ring of the signalman's bell or the rattle of milk churns, but no other signs of activity.

On platform 2, for the Endover service, fireman Harry enjoys his snap and checks the rather depressing racing results, while on platform 1, they are arguing as to whose turn it is to water the hanging baskets.

The foreman keeps his ferrets in the alleyway behind the shed.

There are long pauses when nothing much seems to happen, then sudden flurries of activity at different places in the yard. Coal, of course, but potatoes, corn and cabbages, bicycles, animal feedstuff, cattle, timber, and furniture—the goods clerk was kept busy, monitoring goods in, goods out, goods for collection, goods for delivery, all subject to different rates and prices—endless paperwork.

The goods shed and the coal drops. The goods agent knows the fortunes of every business in town; it all passes through his hands.

Horses were used for shunting until the Second World War—the wagons were much lighter then—and for local cartage. They were stabled in the station yard.

Helen is turned for the return trip, then takes up her position at the head of the train to await the signal to depart.

The guard has put a couple of baskets of strawberries and a bicycle into the brake van, the big gates swing open, the signal drops, and even the cows eye the line with a sort of bleary interest as the train moves slowly forward. It clears the platform, crosses the road, and runs onto the bridge. The exhaust beat quickens then dies away as the tail lamp disappears around the curve. The signal bounces back to danger, the gates close, the cows have gone back to grazing again, and life returns to its normal unhurried pace as the excitement dies away.

Ambleden

The iconic twin spires of St David's Church and the ruins of Ambleden Castle look down over the roof tops of Ambleden.

Such breath-taking views have been secured by our intrepid photographer, but only at considerable risk.

For the more timid, the view from an upstairs window must suffice.

For the really nervous, best stay on the ground …　　　　　*… but watch your step.*

The narrow street, lined with old timber-framed houses and shops, leads down past the covered butter market, where women would come to barter, buy, and sell homemade clothes, dairy produce, and old toys as well as catch up on the local news. The street runs down to the New Victoria Tea Rooms at the bottom of the hill, and to the welcome aroma of newly baked bread and hot coffee—and, of course, horses. The crossing sweeper really was essential.

Fine old houses along East Street. On the left are the premises of Ivor Tome, antiquarian bookseller, with the town assembly rooms above—a popular meeting place when it is not too cold. The Hansom waits outside Floyds Grocers and Poultry Shop, doubtless hoping for a 'shopping-laden' fare.

The Chequers Inn, and a welcome delivery by the drayman of the renowned Amber Ale.

The Sun Inn, still coming to terms with the canal, cut past the front door just 100 years ago.

Rev. Wilson freewheels over the bridge on his way to evensong.

Along the Cut, on the Ambleden Canal

'Beside the towpath, willow veiled,
Slide the heavy barges trailed
By slow horses, and all un-hailed,
The boatmen pass us, tiller-tailed,
Winding down to Camelot.'

Prince trails narrow-boat *Jean* along the cut towards Ambleden. The canal has lost most of its traffic to the railway, but the occasional boat 'winds down to Camelot'—or, rather, Ambleden.

The boatman's wife leads *Prince* along the towpath while the boatman holds the tiller. Working the boats was very much a family affair, with husband and wife and often children living on the boat. On arrival at Ambleden, the boatman will probably call into the Sun Inn 'to register his arrival', while his wife prepares the dinner.

The dominance of the railway overshadows the canal, and it is easy to forget the huge impact that they had when first built in the 1760s. While a horse could pull only a couple of tons on the roadway, it could move some 70 tons on the water, the commercial consequences of which were obvious.

The bridge carrying the towpath over the water outside the Sun Inn. The smooth curves of the masonry were shaped to avoid snagging the tow ropes.

Ambleden Quayside.

George's Lock.

The lock keeper snatches
forty winks while his son,
who tends to overdress the
part, holds the fort.

Prince trails Jean back up the cut to tie up for the night and signals the end of our tour of Amberdale.

While the boatman settles Prince for the night, the smell of hot bacon drifts over the still water, and a solitary owl hoots in the distance. We might just have time to nip back to the Chequers. It is still open.

'What spires, what farms are those?
That is the land of lost content, I see it shining plain,
The happy highways where I went, and cannot come again.'

Trainspotting in Amberdale

I remember my trainspotting days very well—long, carefree summer holiday days, out on my bike in the country to see what we could find. An Ian Allan loco-spotters book (one of the *ABC* books), a timetable, a map, a bottle of ginger beer, and some sandwiches, all squeezed into the saddle bag. Also, of course, I took my camera. By today's standards, it was not up to much. You looked down into the viewfinder, and it had just two settings—bright or cloudy. I never found any difference between them. The film went to the local chemist for processing, and after seven to ten days (sometimes even longer in the summer), an envelope containing about a dozen 2-inch square, rather indistinct black and white contact prints, was the reward.

With Amberdale stretching out before us, it is tempting to venture back into the dale with the help of more up-to-date technology and—it would have seemed impossible then—full colour. Here is a selection of lineside snaps of the railway, the sort of pictures I had hoped to take back then, but never could.

Broad Hambury arrival.

Helen *coasting down the hill. Speeds in excess of 50 mph have been recorded along this stretch of line, presumably when the authorities were not looking.*

Sam *pulls into Ambleden with the baggage car.*

Shunting at Broad Hambury.

Preserved locomotive Hazel, *with a special chartered by the Wenly Miniature Engineering Society, prepares to set off from Wenly on a summer Sunday afternoon. After a number of stops for 'photography' purposes—actually to raise rather more steam—she finally arrives in Ambleden.*

Ethan—*an articulated Garratt locomotive, the most powerful on the line—gets heavy coal on the move from Kingslake Colliery. She fits the Wenly turntable, but only just.*

The chief engineer's private inspection saloon. 'The chief' makes regular tours of the line, checking everything from earthworks to shift schedules, from goods receipts to toilet pennies.

Onich, *with a parcels train, creeps into platform 1 at Wenly, under the watchful eye of the wheel tapper.*

RACING EMILY

Leaving south yard, Wenly, with a mixed goods service.

A brief stop at Kingslake to drop off a horse box.

Crossing the Sorrel and starting the long climb to Ambleden.

… And over the canal.

High above the Amber …

(It was hard work, but I managed to keep ahead of the train the whole way.
The sandwiches and the ginger beer had to wait.)

It's 'Goodbye to all that'

Chloe sets off on the return trip to Chutney, the *Amber Arrow* waits to depart on her return journey from Ambleden to Wenly, and we set off for home. Our photographic expedition has covered quite a lot of ground—we have finally eaten all the sandwiches and finished the ginger beer, and, hopefully, have some good pictures to mull over when we get back.

All the excitement, wonder, drama, and romance of the railway—the noise, the smell, the sense of anticipation, even the taste of the refreshment-room sandwiches.

It is all captured on film, from the days of the Box Brownie, to the digital cameras of today.

What an adventure it has been.

Some Words of Explanation

This is not a book about model railways, nor is it a book showing how to build them, but looking back over the sixty years of its building, and with the enormous benefit of hindsight, a number of lessons have been learned along the way that may be of interest to others starting out on the journey. It would, I think, be disingenuous not to include some description of the model in reality, how it is displayed, and how it all fits together.

Perhaps the most important conclusion is the need to have a firm and clear idea of just what you are trying to achieve. I wanted to build a model of a railway, inspired by but not copied from the Madder Valley, as near as possible to the standards displayed in the Pendon Museum. It was to conjure up the impressions, memories, and atmosphere of the railways I once knew into a convincing three-dimensional picture that would sustain operational interest. The essence of a model railway is that it should 'work' and that it should be worked. The traditional arrangement of a single station connected to hidden storage tracks seemed to offer very limited operational interest that would soon pall, while a railway connecting separate places together and providing for the interchange of traffic between them, just as a real railway does, offered far greater potential. Of course, in the beginning, resources were strictly limited and a model of a complete railway was a distant dream—I lived in a caravan on a construction site—but a railway has to start from somewhere, so work commenced at Ambleden, the terminus of the projected line, and then extended over the years, through the landscape to Wenly, as space and time permitted.

Good intentions and ambitious aspirations are important, but the practical limitations of skill and time will determine what can actually be achieved. I soon discovered that, for me anyway, modelling to consistent standards, whatever those standards might be, was actually more important than striving to achieve what might be termed the 'clinical excellence' of modelling perfection. I learned to accept a standard of modelling skill that was compatible with what I wanted to achieve overall—not, perhaps, as high as I would like, but a sound practical compromise.

Over the years since construction began, there have been huge changes and developments in the modelling world—new materials and equipment, new procedures, and new ideas—and it is reasonable to suppose that such changes will continue into the future. When the building of a model extends over many years, as this one does, there might be a tendency (or a worry) that more recent work will show up the imperfections in the less sophisticated models which were built in the past.

To take an example, all the window frames in Amberdale have been made from layers of paper, fretted out with a fine-bladed craft knife. These days, there is a huge range of ready-made frames laser cut in thin metal, which are, in themselves, a huge improvement on fretted paper, but which, if now introduced into the Amberdale scene, would show up the older models as crude in comparison. By keeping to the long-established, albeit less precise standards, the new frames have not been introduced and the comparison does not arise. Provided the adopted standards remain acceptable, all is well. It may be that those standards can be achieved more readily than hitherto, using new materials and techniques, and it would be a shame not to take advantage of them, but consistency in the appearance of the models is the determining factor.

Amberdale is extremely fortunate in that, by courtesy of the domestic authorities, it has graduated from its caravan origins to a room of its own. The attached double garage was divided up, reasonably amicably, between Amberdale and a utility room. The model is built round the walls of the room at a height of 4 feet above the floor, with the top of the 'sky' about 18 inches above that. It is significantly higher than normal table-top height, such that from a standing view, the models are seen in elevation, rather than in plan; it is a very convenient height at which to work and affords easy access to the underside. The only window in the room is above the 'sky', so that it does not interrupt the continuity of the scene.

The landscape is lit by a continuous neon strip light concealed behind a fascia, which is directly above the front edge of the base board, while a ceiling of polystyrene tiles behind the fascia prevents light spilling out from above. The walls of the room are otherwise dark blue, so the model is displayed as a brightly lit scene around the walls of a dark room. Free of distractions, it commands attention, setting off the model to its best advantage. My workbench, complete with its lighting, slides out from under the base board when required.

The staging of Amberdale harks back to Beal's West Midland and its impression on my boyhood imagination. His dedicated rooms and raised base boards were very much part of the overall spell, in contrast to my railway lines spread out on the carpet—one day, I thought, one day.

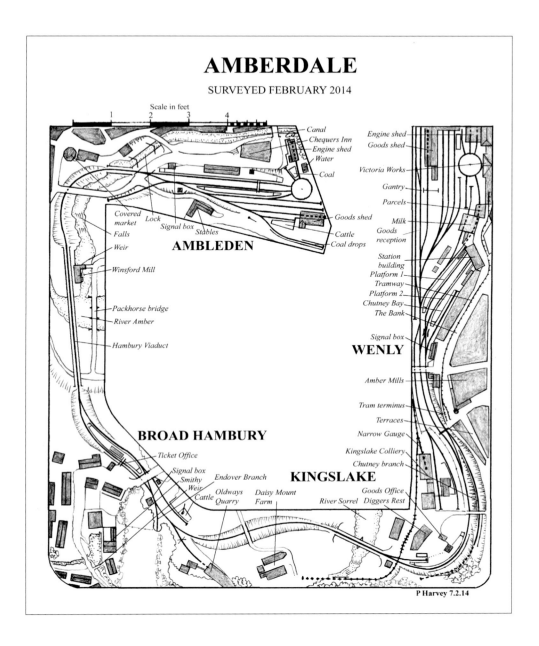

AMBERDALE

SURVEYED FEBRUARY 2014

Scale in feet

Canal
Chequers Inn
Engine shed
Water

Coal

Engine shed
Goods shed

Victoria Works

Gantry

Parcels

Covered market *Lock*
Falls
Signal box *Stables*

AMBLEDEN

Goods shed

Cattle
Coal drops

Milk
Goods reception

Weir

Winsford Mill

Station building
Platform 1
Tramway
Platform 2
Chutney Bay
The Bank

Packhorse bridge
River Amber

Hambury Viaduct

Signal box

WENLY

Amber Mills

Tram terminus
Terraces
Narrow Gauge

BROAD HAMBURY

Ticket Office

Kingslake Colliery
Chutney branch

Signal box
Smithy
Weir
Cattle

Endover Branch

KINGSLAKE

Oldways Quarry
Daisy Mount Farm

Goods Office
River Sorrel *Diggers Rest*

P Harvey 7.2.14

The diagram above shows the railway as it is displayed, while the second shows the concealed lines that enable it to be worked in the desired manner, as explained below.

Ambleden is the market town at the end of the line. From the station, the single line crosses the canal and then Hambury Viaduct, passing over Winsford Mill, before running into Broad Hambury. This station has a loop line enabling trains to pass each other and is the junction for the branch line to the Endovers, which are represented by storage sidings hidden under the village. After passing the small goods yard and Oldways Quarry, the line winds through the countryside to cross the River Sorrel at Kingslake. From here, accompanied by the branch line from Chutney, it skirts the colliery before entering Wenly station.

A narrow-gauge line runs from the colliery to a further siding hidden beyond the river, crossing the main line outside Kingslake station. At Wenly are the main locomotive sheds and workshops, the goods shed, the milk bay, and marshalling and storage sidings, the headquarters of the railway. While the Chutney branch terminates in the bay platform, the main line continues through the platforms to yet more hidden sidings representing the rest of the railway system. An electric tramway through the streets connects the station with the terminus at Amber Mills. There is plenty here to sustain operational interest.

The fundamental difficulty inherent in building a model of a railway is finding the space to separate the stations in a credible way. Scaled up, the distance from one side of the door to the other is less than two-thirds of a mile, and that has to include the length of the stations themselves and their respective communities. Short trains, like those which ran on the Exe Valley and the Sidmouth branch lines, are the answer. Short trains allow short platforms, and short platforms allow short stations.

The station at Wenly has been shortened still further by laying it diagonally across the base board and by having the platforms appearing to continue on under the station building. Having established the minimum length of each station, the task then is to maximise the apparent distance between them. I have concluded that it is not the linear distance between the stations that matters, but the apparent separation. This harks back to my memories of trips to school on the Exe Valley, recalling that my impression of the extent of the line was conditioned not by its length on the map, but instead by the number of stations that separated Exeter from Dulverton.

So here in Amberdale, there are features of dominant interest between the stations, diverting attention away from the railway line and stations themselves. A train arriving at Broad Hambury has not just come from Ambleden; it has just come from crossing the viaduct, the most recent scene that commanded our attention, and Ambleden station has receded into the past, into the distance, out of mind. The apparent distance between the stations is further increased by the suggestion of physical separation, by the wide Amber Valley between Ambleden and Broad Hambury, and between Broad Hambury and Kingslake by the quarry, the cuttings which actually hide the trains from view, and the River Sorrel. We can feel that the stations could not be seen from each other, and that the towns and villages really are some distance apart.

'Off-stage' storage sidings are almost essential to sustain operational interest, allowing trains to be despatched from, stored, and returned to the displayed scene. The trains might be considered as performers, acting in a staged setting, and if attention is diverted from the setting, the illusion is lost, like looking into the wings at the theatre. The necessary facilities are therefore best concealed, out of view, and located under the fully modelled landscape so that they do not use up precious real estate. The second diagram shows how this has been arranged. Trains dispatched from Broad Hambury to the Endovers disappear into a tunnel, where they are reversed on a Wye before backing into store, ready to re-emerge when called as an arrival. Trains departing from Wenly are turned round on the loop line under Broad Hambury. Beyond initiating arrival or departure, all the 'off-stage' storage operates entirely automatically and diverts no attention from the 'front-of-house' scene.

Fostering the illusion also involves simplifying control as far as possible, since manipulating numerous switches was never part of the attraction of watching the real railways and, above all, avoiding the imposition into the scene of that ultimate spoiler, an enormous human hand. These good intentions have been achieved by a degree of simple automation, worked by numerous switches, relays, miniature diodes, and a great deal of wire—but it works.

Having chosen the route, the trains do the rest. The signals come off, the level crossing gates open and close, the automatic couplings couple and uncouple as and when required, and no conflicting routes are set up. In fact, driving the trains might be considered rather dull, but watching them running through the Amberdale countryside is, to me, sufficiently convincing to conjure up and remind me of the impressions and enjoyment I once had from the real thing.

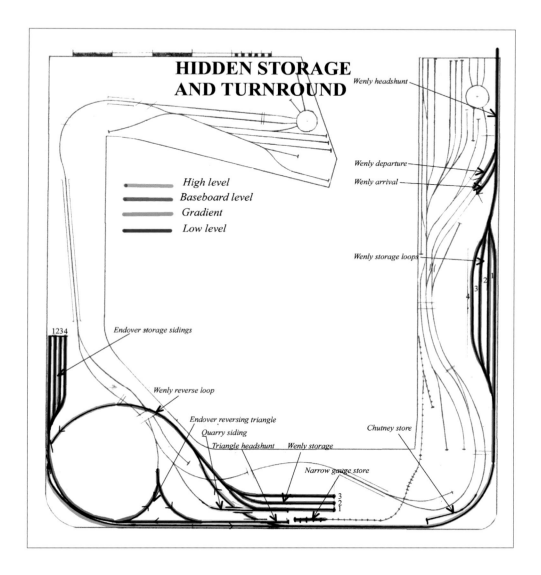

HIDDEN STORAGE AND TURNROUND

Wenly headshunt

Wenly departure

Wenly arrival

High level
Baseboard level
Gradient
Low level

Wenly storage loops

Endover storage sidings

1234

Wenly reverse loop

Endover reversing triangle
Quarry siding

Chutney store

Triangle headshunt   Wenly storage

Narrow gauge store

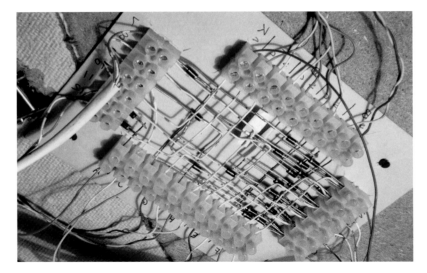

Hmm…

an awful lot of wire…

…but it works.

Notes on the Photographs

Taking the pictures has been as absorbing and as much fun as building the models. The oldest date from about 1975, taken with a very basic Zenith SLR. This much-loved camera was cheap enough to risk experimenting with, so I did and learned a lot—dealing with colour film and colour filters, stopping right down with a pinhole mask over the iris, tilting the lens (with blue tack), and using a mirror. I learned the critical importance of depth of field, with some exposures lasting up to eight minutes. I always used transparency film and found the long wait between the exposure and the processed pictures frustrating in the extreme, though my earlier experience with my box camera in the 1940s should have prepared me.

It all changed with digital cameras of course, exposures took care of themselves, and best of all each picture was open to immediate inspection—and correction. The photographs in this book are a mixture from the earlier film and more recent digital cameras, perhaps most taken with my current Canon Powershot, a miniature camera with a resolution of 12.2 mega-pixels and a minimum aperture of f8. They are taken under the permanent strip lighting fixed above the model. I do not claim any particular expertise or technical knowledge of photography, but I will admit to having acquired some considerable experience of taking pictures of Amberdale.

Two points might be mentioned. The viewpoint, the position of the camera relative to the subject, is critical to taking a 'realistic' picture. A real, full-sized building, seen or photographed from a balloon, looks like a model, and so does a model, however accurate a model it might be. To appear convincing, the picture must be taken from where a 'real' photographer might have taken it. Generally, this means getting down low, which can be difficult in a miniature landscape.

A trick I often use is to take the picture through a mirror propped up next to the subject. By tilting the mirror and positioning the camera accordingly, we can get right down on the ground. The mirror should be front silvered to avoid what would otherwise be a secondary reflection from the surface of the glass. With the film camera and an ordinary mirror, I found I needed to add about half a stop to compensate for the surface reflection. Of course, the image will be reversed in the mirror, but that can be easily corrected in the computer. In the old film days, the correction was made simply by turning the transparency over, but I struggled to persuade the processing people to take prints from the wrong side of the film.

The mirror propped up behind the carriage, tilted well back.

Here is the picture acutally being taken by the camera.

In this third picture, the image has been flipped over to correct the reflection. It has been cropped and the 'top' of the sky replaced with a 'real' one.

The other difficulty is the sky. While Amberdale is built in front of a permanent sky back cloth, it is only effective when viewed from immediately in front. If the camera is tilted upwards, or aimed from behind towards the front of the model, then the pictures show either the top of the sky or no sky at all. To overcome this difficulty, I have grafted photographs of real skies onto many of the pictures, again in the computer. Care has to be taken to match the perspective and lighting of the sky to that of the subject, but it adds significantly to the realism of the finished picture. I have used a similar procedure to mask the front edge of the base board, where it would otherwise intrude into the picture, by grafting on a suitable foreground chosen from some other part of the model. Baseboard edges in the foreground, and large coffee cups in the background, are to be avoided at all costs if the pictures are to carry conviction.

Here the camera is aimed towards the front of the model, showing the door to the room. The superimposed 'real' sky helps considerably.

These notes pick out some points of interest in the photographs—the facts, rather than the fiction—and are, of course, written with the benefit of hindsight.

The Amber Valley

The photographs in this book are intended to show the railway as an element of the larger landscape, and as subordinate to it. So these introductory pictures are as rural as possible, deliberately avoiding any hint of the railway. The wide-open spaces of Amberdale cannot be modelled within the confines of the railway room, so they have to be suggested on the painted back scene. The leading panorama is the scene behind Kingslake, while the gull emphasises the bird's eye view, which is how the model is first seen in reality, spread out round the walls of the room.

The pictures of the river are taken from a sequence illustrating Tennyson's poem 'The Brook', which many of us remember. Photographing to what might be described as a menu, as opposed to taking random snapshots, can result in otherwise unimagined views of the so familiar scene. The effective portrayal of water depends largely on the selection and modelling of the immediate surroundings, the river banks, bridges, overhanging trees, and so forth. The assorted livestock, fish, swans, and cows reinforce the impression of a water surface and add a focal point to the pictures. The distant shot of St David's Church is a montage of pictures taken of Amberdale, but put together 'not necessarily in the right order'. The reeds in front of the stone bridge mask the edge of the base board and are represented by a piece of turf from the garden. It was put back afterwards.

Broad Hambury

The ground rises up towards the White Swan at the far end of the village, the buildings built progressively to a slightly smaller scale as they recede. The reduction in size and the significant depth of field suggests real distance up the main street. Obtaining a realistic reflection from the surface of the pond was not easy. The scene beyond has to be brightly lit, particularly the sky, but with fixed lighting and a painted sky.

The false perspective of the church tower is modelled in low relief. The strong horizontal roof line in front of it serves as a sort of eye level base line from which the perspective can be set out. The picture through the cottage window was taken with the old film camera. A window was modelled to a suitable scale, then a transparency of the garden was propped up tight behind it and back lit, such that both the window and the garden would be in focus. It would be far easier to do it today using the computer and would actually be better if the window was slightly out of focus, as it would be in a full-size situation. There is a danger in that the computer and the digital camera may enable us to produce pictures that would have been unachievable with ordinary film cameras, and that might be less convincing in consequence. Gray's Elegy was too good to miss, though the position of the setting sun suggests that the tower is at the wrong end of the church.

Broad Hambury Station

Depth of field and a low-level viewpoint conjure up an impressive sense of space. The pictures are composed to ensure that our view does not extend far beyond the station, which might show that the next station is not very far away. It was tempting to include the top of the parapet in the view looking down onto the platform from the bridge, justifying the high viewpoint—beware 'balloon' shots. Yet of course, in a real-life situation, one would have been careful to avoid such out-of-focus stonework intruding into the picture.

Oldways Quarry

The extensive working face of the quarry is, fortunately, out of sight behind the main buildings, there would never be room for it otherwise. The view across the fields shows the merging of the solid modelled foreground into the painted background, mainly a matter of adjusting the intensity of the shadows between the two surfaces. This picture illustrates the importance of sky perspective. Clouds over the hill just do not look like that.

Hambury Viaduct

This is a major feature on the line, and measures were taken to make it suitably spectacular. The whole structure is built to a reduced scale, about 3 mm to the foot rather than 4 mm elsewhere. This enables a model of a larger and therefore more impressive structure to be fitted into the available space. The reduced scale is not immediately apparent because the trains running over it are short and the locomotives small.

The viaduct is not built parallel to the edge of the base board, and is positioned and lit so that its shadow does not fall on the back scene or the sky, but on the ground beneath. The back scene itself is composed such that the left-hand end is darker than the structure, receding behind it, while the right-hand end is lighter, showing the model against it in silhouette. Similarly, the approaches on either side are completely different, with a cutting at one end and an embankment at the other. The contrast between the two ends increases the apparent length of the structure. The height is emphasised by the low stone bridge in the immediate foreground, which also restricts the low-level view upstream to where the surface of the river turns up through 90 degrees to meet the back scene.

This latter ploy increases the effective length of the river as seen from the normal viewing position. The height is further accentuated by the railway running clearly above the tree tops and the roof of the mill far below. The water mill and its rotating wheel draw the eye down from the high girders, emphasising still further the height as it 'strides across the landscape'. The most difficult part of the scene to compose was the need to make the back scene behind the dropped base board compatible with that at the higher level on either side—shades of the Wye Valley here. When I first took the view through the trees, using the old film camera, I arranged half the garden in front of it, to mask the base board and simulate depth of field. It was a lot easier using the computer.

Winsford Mill

The wheel is driven through a double worm reduction gearbox to turn at about 8 rpm. The water tumbling off the wheel is cotton wool, positioned just clear of the rotating paddles—not as effective as I would like, but certainly more convincing than real water and a lot easier to arrange. The low-level view of the wheel took the best part of a day to photograph, involving reflections through two mirrors and some aching muscles, but I was pleased with the result. It is, of course, quite impossible to view the actual model from that angle.

The everyday views of Amberdale have inevitably, after some sixty years, become very, very, familiar, so it is always exciting when the camera is able reveal a completely fresh and hitherto unseen aspect of the model.

Along the Valley Road

A pleasant contrast to the railway. There are more than sixty horse-drawn vehicles in the dale, all scratch built with full under gear and, where appropriate, upholstered interiors. Much more attractive than motor cars, they have been copied from drawings or photographs, or measured up in museums. The fore carriages of the four-wheeled vehicles are pivoted to rotate and tilt so that they can be realistically posed on rough roads with all wheels firmly on the ground. The Surrey with the fringe on top is my favourite, inspired by Oscar Hammerstein's *Oklahoma*. The Surrey was very much an American carriage; they were equi-rotal—all the wheels were the same size. In the wide-open spaces of the American West, manoeuvrability was not a problem. I have anglicised it by reducing the diameter of the front wheels. The post-chaise must be getting on a bit now, though as a very expensive carriage for its time, it would have been looked after very carefully. This one was.

On the Land

Hopefully, these pictures do not reveal too obviously the dimensional liberties taken in building the models. The trees are far too small. Trees in Amberdale are generally about 6 inches high. If built to scale, they would be about twice that height, but it would then make the surrounding landscape seem very much smaller and confined. Provided they are consistent, the reduced size is acceptable. The barn is also far too small; it again should be about twice the size, and the pantiles on its roof are too large. The building as modelled is only about '60 tiles' long overall, so something is seriously adrift somewhere. And yet… and yet… despite the gross inaccuracies, the pictures are still sufficiently convincing, at least to me. Colouring, texture, subject, and composition are, perhaps, more important in that respect than clinical accuracy.

The Coming of the Railway

Some fun with old Victorian photographs—combining photos of models with photos of the real thing can be tricky. As we look through pictures such as the ones in this book, we tend to lose touch with the real world and accept their portrayal as the reality. However, if a picture of, for example, a real tree was to be suddenly introduced into the sequence, it would be hugely discordant, with the comparison showing how unreal the modelled ones actually are. But the old photos of people do not conflict with the modelled surroundings; there is no direct comparison, so these combined pictures work quite well.

The Railway Today

Pictures emphasising the rural nature of the line suggest that there might be a real distance between the stations. Super-imposing some foreground foliage is, I suppose, cheating, but it helps set the scene. In such cases, the overhanging trees are far enough away from those modelled in the background to avoid the comparison referred to above.

The *Amber Arrow* was inspired by a well-remembered trip on the *Devon Belle* shortly after the war, though I cannot recall the actual menu. This is what it might have been. I have some doubts about the curved quarter lights at the end of the observation car; could they have been manufactured back in the 1890s? I think they are more attractive than the squared-off windows of the actual vehicle. The Pullman carriages are, needless to say, far too short, but with their lined-out yellow and brown liveries, elliptical vestibule windows, brass handrails, individual names, table lamps, and white roofs, they look like Pullman cars to me—a long way, though, from being scale models.

From Broad Hambury to Kingslake

The most convincing pictures tend to be those showing the most commonplace, most ordinary, subjects. A small nondescript tank engine pulling a few wooden coaches through an unremarkable landscape has an air of familiarity about it, which prompts lazy acceptance of the pictures, rather than their detailed critical analysis. And was the small wayside station ever better described than by Edward Thomas?

We must assume that the River Sorrel has changed course over the last twenty years or so, since the engineers who built it would surely not have sited the centre pier of the bridge in the middle of the stream. The severity of the gradient up the line to Broad Hambury is evidenced in the courses of masonry just below the parapet.

Kingslake

The layout of the station and the village was designed to conceal, so far as possible, the very sharp curve that takes the railway round the corner of the room and also hide the end of the Chutney branch—it is under the bank behind the platform.

The back scene is swept around the corner in a curve, and the 'dip' in the hills on the skyline reduces still further the prominence of the corner, seen from normal viewing height. The row of small terrace houses has been built in forced perspective. This sort of distortion can be quite effective, provided the view point is suitably restricted, say by other buildings or trees. In this case, the corner of the room prevents the row from being seen from the right, such that the smaller 'distant' end would be closer to the observer than the larger near end. The detailing of the buildings is progressively

reduced as they recede. The terrace climbs a hill into the distance—an essential ploy to maintain the overall roof line, otherwise the scene would appear to recede downhill as the buildings become smaller. The gradient complicates the perspective and widens the acceptable viewpoint.

Kingslake Colliery

Collieries are large and complex, and modelling one is not easy. Either most of it has to be represented on the back scene or it has to be a very small colliery. The one here at Kingslake falls into the latter category. It includes just those features that comprise the essence of a colliery in the popular imagination—the engine house and head gear, the boiler house, the loading screens, some pit props, and some coal.

Once again, the head gear is too small, but if built accurately to scale, it would take up more space than is available and dominate the scene. The front of the engine house lifts off to reveal the working engine inside, whilst the interior of the screening building is exposed by lifting off the roof. Modelling interiors is fun but they are not 'on view', so to some extent wasted, though they are of course known to the builder and to the camera. Those modelled at Pendon are actually displayed outside their respective buildings. I was determined to have some narrow gauge in somewhere, so here it is. The view of the grassy track winding away between the buildings, with the lonely hopper wagon rusting in the sun, is iconic. The locomotive is obviously based on the Darjeeling prototype, but I have added a pony truck to improve pick up. The wheel base was adjusted to ensure that never more than one axle would span the rail gaps where the line crosses the standard gauge, again to ensure reliable pick up. I accept that the rear axle now fouls the firebox—or *vice versa*; it is on my 'to-do' list.

Wenly

While in villages like Broad Hambury, low cottages and their gardens can spread out; in an urban setting, the buildings need to be much closer together and taller, with several more floors, suggesting that space is restricted. From a modelling point of view, the height of the buildings must be limited, just as is that of the trees in the countryside, to maximise the apparent area of the scene. Additional floors can be added by putting them under the roof, lit by dormer windows and roof lights, such that the overall height of the building is not increased. At the same time, because they are normally seen from above, the roofs of model buildings are far more dominant than those of real buildings seen from below, so the greater the variety in their design, the more interesting and attractive the townscape will appear. These two factors explain the 'roofscape' of Wenly.

The colouring is also important. The urban scene needs to have a sort of dull uniformity of tone, suggestive of smoke, fog, and what might be termed 'industrial decay'—no bright colours or harsh contrasts and a very restricted palette, mainly greys and browns. Cloudy grey skies make a change from the blue normally seen over most model railways, and are perhaps more compatible with the industrial or urban scene.

The chimney of Amber Mills towers over the town. As factory chimneys go, it is not very tall—tiny, in fact. A medium-sized mill chimney would scale down to about 3 feet 6 inches; it would be substantially higher than the top of the 'sky'. Some sort of compromise is necessary. It is all a matter of proportion. Here the height is such that, from the normal viewing position, some sky is visible above the top of the chimney, and the top is above eye level so we have to look upwards to see it. The mill itself, though large compared to the adjacent buildings, is substantially smaller than it really should be, so the proportions of the shorter chimney seem acceptable. Care was taken to ensure that the shadow of the chimney does not fall on the sky.

The Tramway

3-foot gauge track was adopted, rather than standard gauge, as less demanding of street space. The two tram cars are scratch built with the motors and drive trains concealed under the floor so that the interior can be fully modelled. Pick up is from the track, the overhead wiring is not live. The pick-up pole is spring-loaded against the conductor wire and is arranged to flip over automatically for the return trip, which happens after the car has disappeared behind suitably placed buildings. With only four wheels, the pick up from the rails has been augmented by the addition of collector shoes hidden under the bodywork, and by a network of miniature diodes hidden under the lower deck seats which drop the voltage from the track to the motor. The trams run at an acceptably slow speed, pausing twice on their journey from the terminus to the station.

Wenly Station

While in theory the station continues on under the bridge, in fact the platforms stop abruptly and the tracks curve away sharply into the hidden kick back. This subterfuge has been masked by painting everything under the bridge black, by positioning a prominent girder support column in the middle of the span, and by placing pale painted lattice girders across the tracks between the platform canopies. From normal viewing angles, these effectively block the view into the void. The scene over the bridge behind the station building is suggestive of the platforms continuing on, complete with a working departure signal showing above the parapet.

Wenly South Yard

The left-hand end of the base board is closed off with a mirror. It increases substantially the apparent size of the scene and avoids the squared-off end of the base board, which would otherwise emphasise the table-top appearance of many model railways.

The mirror extends from the works foundry chimney in the middle of the sawtooth roof to the extreme left of the picture. The chimney conceals the join between the mirror and the sky behind the station, which would otherwise appear in the corner as a dark vertical line the thickness of the glass. Buildings, the engine sheds, water tower, and goods shed are arranged along the base of the mirror so that the railway tracks and their moving trains are not reflected back to the observer. A train seen approaching itself along a single line would look odd to say the least.

Ensuring that the reflected image makes sense is quite entertaining, such as lettering down a factory chimney, using letters with a vertical axis of symmetry—TIMOTHY, for example—and painting chimney pots a different colour on the side immediately adjacent to the mirror, so that it reflects as a different pot. Paradoxically, the more inconspicuous the mirror, the more effective it is. Often, visitors to Amberdale do not notice it at all, until it is pointed out to them.

The view in the mirror has been covered over in the second picture to show the actual extent of the modelling.

Smoke and Steam at Wenly MPD

The row of buildings in the background conceals the kick-back line, which gives access to the hidden storage sidings under the town. The design of the buildings is intended to discourage any idea that a railway line is hidden behind them. Thus, the prominent archway over the entrance to Victoria Works, the varying roof line, and the irregular frontages of the building suggest that there would be insufficient room for a rail track. The locomotive emerging from the works entrance is, of course, posing without its tender.

Wenly to Ambleden

Some of these pictures show the Chutney branch line as it climbs away into the hills. The rising gradient gives visual emphasis to the line, a more interesting and attractive arrangement than had it been kept on the level. It also slows the departing train as it climbs the bank, increasing the effect of distance. The cows, of course, are an everyday hazard one just has to accept.

Ambleden Station

The location of the turntable might be questioned, but I am sure there will have been a precedent for it somewhere, it certainly saves space. I am not so sure, though, about the floor of the signal cabin being jetted out over the locking room, but it makes an attractive model. I must have seen something like it somewhere. The twin spires of St David's really do seem to be some way away.

Ambleden

Distorted perspective, varying scales and ground levels, graduated low relief modelling, and multi-layered backgrounds were all deployed to make the most of limited space. Ambleden was the first townscape to be tackled, so it served as the proving ground to explore and develop these techniques. Early rules laid down by the management provided that no ground was to be at rail level other than for the actual track itself and that no area of any size should be flat, countering the table-top appearance of many model railways. Ambleden, Wenly, Kingslake, and Broad Hambury are all built on hills and look the better for it.

Journey's End

The stained-glass east window of St David's shows up well, lit through the non-existent roof panel. Quite how that light could flood into the church in reality, though, is not clear. This is an invented memory. While it may seem vaguely familiar, there could never have been a scene like this.

Conclusions

So that is Amberdale. It is just sixty years since it began, since the platforms at Ambleden were built. Over that time, it has been subject, quite properly, to the priorities of earning a living and normal family life, to the counter attractions of other interests, to holidays and moving house, to a succession of dogs and cats—of cats, the least said the better. For all that, goodness knows how many hours have been spent in the 'railway room'.

It has continued to sustain my interest by virtue of its variety; from engineering to art, from investigation and research to imaginative invention. It has also been fun, challenging, frustrating, and maddening at times, but immensely satisfying due to the simple but intense pleasure of fulfilled enthusiasm, for whatever it might be—in this case, for making things and building models. It has proved to be the perfect distraction from the professional worries that inevitably arise from time to time, and often prompted an answer to them. All those hours have been well spent.

Have I achieved what I set out to do? It is certainly a model of a railway, very much in the tradition of the Madder Valley, but to Pendon standards? Of course not. I soon discovered that, even if I ever acquired the skills, such standards would be incompatible with modelling a complete railway in one lifetime. Fortunately, I also discovered that faithfully modelling every rivet and brick was not necessary, but that a less rigorous, more imaginative approach could be just as effective, provided whatever standards I adopted were common across the entire project. So, accepting that the quality of the modelling is rather less than I originally hoped, I can say that I am satisfied with the result.

How do the pictures in this book compare with those which so enchanted me as a boy? There is no simple answer. The improved technology of today's photographs certainly makes for a much more convincing portrayal of reality, but on the other hand, the rather indistinct nature of the older pictures masked the imperfections in the models and left more to the imagination. I have no doubt that the pictures of Hambury Viaduct compare favourably with Ahern's pictures of his bridge in the hills, though whether they have the same charm is another matter.

I have to confess that over the last year or two actual modelling has tailed off a bit, with more time spent on maintenance, operation, and simple but enjoyable contemplation, particularly since the model has been effectively finished in overall terms. All the ground has been covered, all the trains and horse carriages I planned have been built, though there is still work to be done. Will I finally get around to fitting out Amber Mills with spinning frames and carding machines? It has been on the action list for twenty years at least.

At any time, I can and do wander into the railway room and see the Amberdale of my imagination spread out before me, from the high hills above Hawkridge where the river rises down to the smoking chimneys of Wenly. Press a couple of switches and *Harriet* might come creeping over Hambury Viaduct with a train from the Endovers, or I might choose to watch the water cascading down the tailrace below Winsford Mill while the big wheel turns and sparkles under the elms. I could walk up the hill through Broad Hambury in the sunshine to the White Swan, splash about in the Sorrel under the railway bridge as we used to in the River Otter, or rattle up Wenly's Bank Street in an open top tram.

There are plenty of memories, real and imagined, of long hot summer days, of steam engines and train journeys, of horse carriages and hay rides, and of cottage gardens, canals, corn fields, and country lanes. They are all here, made real, in Amberdale.

A Last Look
Her whistle echoing across the fields,
Emily *pulls away from Kingslake*
to begin the long climb through to
Ambleden. As she disappears around
the curve and the sound dies away,
we can hear the Sorrel rippling under
the bridge and, perhaps, if we listen
very carefully, the song of a solitary
blackbird—just as one was heard, all
those years ago, in Adlestrop.

Postscript

Eagle-eyed readers will have noticed a number of quotations spread through the book. They are mostly of verse, and many have been 'adjusted' to reflect their context, for which I hope I will be forgiven. They are there because they have proved to be sources of inspiration and because they summarise the feelings and aspirations behind the models and pictures more effectively than I can myself. Reminders of long remembered but partly forgotten poetry can provide strong support to the real or imagined memories evoked by the pictures. So grateful acknowledgements to Housman, Auden, Tennyson (twice), Novello, Vera Lynn, Brooke, Gray, Hammerstein, Thomas, Browning, Stevenson, Graves, and Eric Morecambe.

A number of characters in the book are mentioned by name. That these names might correspond with those of people I know is, of course, coincidental. Let's just say they are names I'm pleased to encounter in the dale.